Trerice

CORNWALL

A souvenir guide

National Trust

A GRAND MANOR HOUSE

The Elizabethan manor house of Trerice lies in a peaceful wooded valley not far from what is today the busy popular tourist resort of Newquay. A grand manor 'on a Cornish scale' Trerice has changed little over the centuries due to long periods under absentee landlord-owners.

The Arundells of Trerice

The origins of the Arundells of Trerice are hazy, though the name is of Norman origin. They were cousins of the 'Great Arundells' of Lanherne and may even have been distantly connected to the Norman earls of Arundel. Out of this mist comes Ralph Arundell, who married Jane, daughter and heiress of Michael de Trerise, in the mid-14th century.

The Arundell family owned Trerice for nearly 500 years, though the family often preferred to live elsewhere. Legend has it that John Arundell II moved to Trerice from his coastal manor of Ebbingford to avoid a prophecy foretelling that 'he should be slain in the sands'. At this time Trerice itself was probably not much larger than a farmhouse surrounded by a busy working farm.

Above John Arundell V, rebuilder of Trerice; detail of the family tomb brass in St Andrew's Church, Stratton, north Cornwall

Right The entrance front from the kayling lawn

Fit for a gentleman

During the 16th and 17th centuries the Arundell family prospered through marriage alliances and gaining positions in local government. The present house was completed in 1572-3, around the time of John Arundell V's second marriage, to Gertrude Denys. It incorporated the earlier 14th-century manor house but was rebuilt in the latest fashion, with its curling Dutch gables (among the earliest examples in Britain) and Elizabethan 'E' layout. The remodelling of the house and gardens transformed Trerice into a comfortable residence fit for a leading Cornish gentleman.

Ruin and revival

Trerice passed to the Acland family of Killerton after the Arundell line died out in the mid-18th century, through the marriage of Margaret Acland to John, 2nd Baron Arundell of Trerice. The Acland family owned the estate, which was occupied by tenants, until 1915, when it was sold. It was during this time that the northern end of the house fell into ruin; it finally came down after a gale in the 1860s. The County Council bought it in 1919 and divided up much of the land into individual farms and tenancies. In 1953 Trerice was bought by the National Trust, and due to the generosity of the tenant, Mr J.F Elton, the northern end was restored to a semblance of its former self.

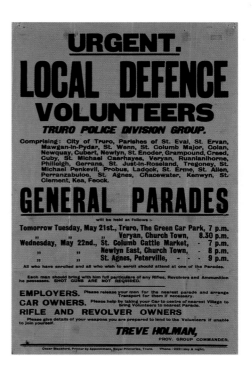

Above Trerice was the headquarters of the local Home Guard during the Second World War

What's in a name?

'Trerice, anciently Treres, offereth you the view of ... costly and commodious buildings. What *Tre* [house] is, you know already, *res* signifieth a rushing or fleeting away, and upon the declining of a hill the house is seated.'

The Survey of Cornwall, 1602; by Richard Carew, historian and son-in-law of John Arundell V.

It is now generally thought that Trerice means 'the settlement by the ford' (the higher tidal reach of the river gave this ford a greater importance than it has now).

Prospect and pleasure

'Nowadays they [the Cornish gentry] seat their dwellings high, build their walls thin, lay them with earthen mortar, raise them to three or four stories, mould their lights large and outward, and their roofs square and slight, coverting chiefly prospect and pleasure. As for glass and plaster for private men's houses, they are of late years' introduction.'

Richard Carew

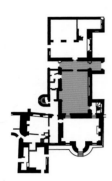

TOUR OF THE HOUSE

THE GREAT HALL

Entering the Great Hall today, it is easy to imagine stepping back in time and to sense the impact it would have made in Tudor times. The size, the height, the plasterwork ceiling and the tiled floor, especially with the light pouring in from the newly glazed window, would have left many visitors awestruck.

A social space

The layout follows the form of medieval times, when the Great Hall was the main room in the manor house, and masters, servants and animals ate, slept and worked together. By the 16th century the family wanted greater privacy, and so its meals and other daily activities took place in other rooms, especially the Great Chamber upstairs. The Great Hall gradually took on a new role, primarily for social occasions.

Great East Window

The large window, rising through two storeys, is the main source of light for the Great Hall. It contains 576 panes, many of which are the original glass. In the 16th century clear glass was imported from Europe and was therefore still an expensive commodity. In the mid-1570s the hall window would have impressed everyone who saw it.

Plasterwork ceiling

The ceiling is a fine example of West Country plasterwork: a large open pattern made up of interlocking thin ribs, ornamented with oak leaves and scrolled designs. At intervals the ceiling is supported by corbels decorated with rudimentary busts set in medallions. The centre of the ceiling echoes Gothic fan vaulting, but has been given a 1570s twist by the addition of spherical pendants. Between the pendants, in the group of four squares, are the initials J.A, K.A. and M.A. These

The Screens Passage
The Screens Passage was used to block out draughts from the main entrance into the Great Hall. It also provided space for a musicians' gallery above, from where the music would waft down to the family and guests below in the Hall.

OPPOSITE

Top The Great Hall

Bottom The plasterwork overmantel

are probably the initials of John Arundell V, who rebuilt the house, and his first wife, Katherine, though these initials were common among several generations of the family. The plasterwork was restored by Sir Thomas Dyke Acland in the 1840s.

Furniture

The long oak refectory table is a 19th-century design inspired by a Tudor table that was originally in the house. It was made with timber from the Aclands' Holnicote estate in Somerset and was the only large piece of furniture acquired with the house in 1953. The National Trust gradually acquired the rest over the following decades.

Fireplace

The plaster overmantel (dated 1572 and supported by male and female terms) was a popular feature in Elizabethan times. The blank cartouche in the middle of the overmantel may have been decorated with the family's coat of arms in paint or plasterwork.

THE DRAWING ROOM

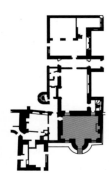

This room is at a lower level than the Hall and the thickness of the walls suggests that this was part of the original medieval dwelling. On entering the room the initial impact is often one of gloom compared with the Hall.

The semi-circular bay may have been added by John Arundell V in the 1570s, and possibly incorporated a spiral turret staircase, which may explain the lack of large windows in this room. The sash-windows date from the early 19th century, when the room was divided up into a dining room (incorporating the bay and French windows) and a breakfast room with the 19th-century fireplace. In 1969 the National Trust removed the partitions and restored the room to its original dimensions. Three years later, the doorway to the left of the fireplace was opened to give direct access to the staircase.

Originally called a 'withdrawing' room, a drawing room was used as an antechamber for private meals or as somewhere a personal servant might sleep. By the late 16th century it had become more like a private sitting room and by the 18th century it was an intimate and cosy alternative to the more formal rooms. With its contrasting low ceiling and soft furnishings, it was often a place where ladies would retire after dinner.

Tunnel

Under the floor is a well-built tunnel. Dating from the 1570s, it once took surface water or water from a nearby spring to a mill leat on the south-west side of the house. It was once thought to be drainage for a garderobe or privy, or, more romantically, a secret priest's hole leading to the orchard.

Staircase

The stairwell occupies part of the Elizabethan façade built by John Arundell V in 1572, and traces of the original, circular stair are said to have been found in the walls. The present staircase was probably installed during the early 19th century.

Margaret Acland

On top of the 18th-century bookcase against the inner wall stands a bust of Margaret Acland (d.1691), who married John Arundell, 2nd Baron Arundell of Trerice in 1675. This marriage united the two families and it was through her that the Acland family inherited Trerice in the early 19th century. The bust is modelled on the one from her tomb in the nearby parish church of St Newlyn East. Margaret's memorial described her as:

long conspicuous for her honours, always for her virtues who, in these recently troubled times was especially distinguished in loyalty and duty towards the King. Her affection towards God, her husband and her children and her services towards all her neighbours was such that they could scarcely be equalled and certain not surpassed. Wives, mothers, friends, everyone weep for her, honour her, strive to emulate her.

Left The Drawing Room

Opposite A Jacobite drinking bowl dated 1745, the year of the last Jacobite rising

THE GREAT CHAMBER

The Great Chamber reflects the aspirations and position of the family in the 1570s. This was the main reception room of the house, an Elizabethan version of the medieval solar. By the 1690s it was known as 'My Lady's Chamber', and used as a drawing room for entertaining visitors as well as a bedroom.

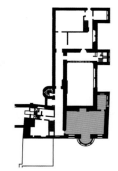

Plasterwork ceiling

The elaborate plaster barrel ceiling is an admirable example of West Country workmanship from the 1570s. Wooden lathes were attached to the underside of the joists, with plaster applied over the top. The plaster pendants were created using a timber frame with plaster moulded around them. The Tudor rose motif was popular in houses during the 16th century.

Windows

Facing south, the large bay window floods the room with light. The ceiling in the bay differs from the pattern in the main room, but repeats the Tudor rose motif. The sash-windows are 19th century. At various times throughout the house's history these windows have been blocked up. A window once in the east wall has been completely removed.

Opposite The Great Chamber

Coat of arms

The coat of arms on the lunette above the plaster frieze on the west wall is that of Henry FitzAlan, 12th and last FitzAlan Earl of Arundel and Knight of the Garter. His second wife was Mary Radcliffe, daughter of Sir John Arundell of Lanherne, a first cousin of 'Jack of Tilbury' (see p.23), through the latter's mother, Jane Grenville. It is also possible that Arundell saw a hazy family connection through the Earl of Arundel to the Norman d'Aubigny earls of Arundel. The use of coats of arms was a popular decorative device, but the Arundells' use of the FitzAlan arms, though boastful, was also a little dangerous, acknowledging links to leading Catholic families at a time when Catholicism was being repressed; and especially after the Ridolfi plot in 1570, which led to the execution in 1572 of the Duke of Norfolk, who had married Mary FitzAlan, step-daughter to Mary Arundell of Lanherne and heiress of the Earl of Arundel.

WEST COUNTRY PLASTERWORK

Trerice is one of a small number of houses in the far South West with plasterwork from the 16th century. The closest examples to Trerice are in Devon and Somerset - at Colleton Barton, in Chumleigh, Collacombe Barton in Lamerton, near Tavistock, and Buckland Abbey, near Plymouth. Many of the designs used, the details of the strapwork, the friezes and pendants are very similar to Trerice. The dates of the plasterwork at all of these properties are quite close – Trerice 1572 and 1573, Collacombe 1574 and Buckland 1576 - suggesting that the same craftsmen may have been responsible. There also seem to have been family connections. John Arundell may have met Edmund Tremayne, builder of Collacombe, through his father Jack of Tilbury, a vice-admiral and sheriff of Cornwall. Tremayne would have known Sir Richard Grenville of Buckland, who was also a distant cousin of Arundell.

It is likely that local plasterers carried out the work rather than continental craftsmen, but they would have been exposed to foreign ideas to decoration through pattern books, which were combined with individual tastes and styles. Strapwork (where the plaster is made to look like curling leather straps) was a type of Flemish ornament which appealed to English taste in the 16th century, and echoes the Dutch influence on the exterior of Trerice. Motifs and symbols with hidden meanings were also popular: oak leaves symbolised strength and power; a vine depicted eternal love or friendship; while a sword depicted justice, and cornucopias symbolised plenty.

The Great Chamber overmantel

The Great Chamber fireplace, like that in the Great Hall, is an important feature of the room, with the overmantel incorporating the family's coat of arms. The arms in the central cartouche belong to John Arundell V's father, 'Jack of Tilbury', flanked by those of his wives' families, Bevill and Erisey. The plasterwork may originally have been brightly painted in the heraldic colours of the families. The overmantel is supported by two classically clothed caryatids, suggesting the family's martial past and its aspirations of elegance and peace. The date of 1573 at the top suggests that this room was finished after the Great Hall and was possibly one of the last rooms to be completed. Perhaps because of poor planning, the craftsman who added the date ran out of room to complete the date in proper Roman style.

CLOCKS

Over the years a varied collection of English clocks has been gathered at Trerice. Among the earliest in the house are clocks by Thomas Tompion (1639–1713), the son of a blacksmith, who was the leading clock and watchmaker at the court of Charles II, and often called the 'Father of English watchmaking'. He adapted the theories of Robert Hooke to improve clock mechanisms, making them equal to the prized craftsmanship of the cases. Among his achievements Tompion made the first clocks used at the Greenwich Observatory in 1676, and the first watch regulated by a balance spring. He became a master of the Clockmakers' Company in 1704.

Edward Banger was nephew by marriage to Thomas Tompion and worked as his apprentice in the 1690s. Between 1701 and 1708 he went into partnership with Tompion. Joseph Knibb (1640–1711), a contemporary of Tompion, was from an Oxfordshire family of clockmakers and also made clocks for Charles II. He was admitted to the Clockmakers' Company in 1670, and is often viewed as one of the few clockmakers of the time to come close to Tompion's craftsmanship and status.

Joseph Windmills of London was made a freeman of the Clockmakers' Company in 1671, and had a number of apprentices including his son Thomas. During their partnership the clocks produced were signed simply 'Windmills'.

Among other notable clocks in the house is a tripod clock with glass dome by Thomas Cole (1800–64), showing the beautiful design work and excellent workmanship for which he was noted. The brass 30-hour striking lantern clock in the Great Hall was made about 1750, almost 50 years after they were fashionable in London, but typical of provincial England. The single-handed clock is driven by weights that need resetting every 30 hours, compared to 17th-century versions that needed winding every eight to twelve hours.

Several of the clocks have their own individual features. The 18th-century longcase clock by Stephen Henry has a particularly distinctive peal of chimes marking each quarter hour. The longcase clock by Robert Wood also marks the lunar calendar above the clock face.

Left Ebony bracket clock by Joseph Knibb

THE LONG GALLERY

The Long Gallery was initially intended as a space for indoor exercise, where ladies would stroll and gossip on wet days, and children could play games. When the National Trust bought Trerice, it was split by two modern staircases. These were removed to restore the long corridor to its original purpose.

Ceiling
The plasterwork ceiling continues the light, airy feeling from the Great Chamber. It has been repaired since it was originally installed.

Arundell charter
This framed document is the Peerage Patent of King Charles II, creating Richard Arundell the first Baron Arundell of Trerice on 23 March 1664/5. Richard, with his father, John, the governor of Pendennis Castle who died in 1656, and his brothers, had distinguished themselves during the Civil War fighting for the Royalist cause. A peerage had been promised in 1646, but was not granted until 1664/5, when the fortunes of the monarch and the Arundell family had recovered.

According to the document, Richard Arundell *'had fought fiercely, repeatedly wounded in battles and siege and his dutiful purpose and that of his brothers did not falter although their homes were attacked and stormed and …on no occasion forsook the kingdom nor deserted the lost King'*.

Left The Long Gallery

THE MUSICIANS' GALLERY

The high openings on the south wall were intended to allow the sound from musicians to permeate into the Great Hall below. Crumhorns, shawms, tabors and lutes were popular instruments during the 16th century, and would be played while the family ate below or for dancing and festive occasions.

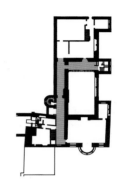

EMBROIDERY

Stumpwork

Raised work or stumpwork was a popular form of needlework in the 16th and 17th centuries, and was used to decorate clothes as well as furnishings. Engravings of Biblical scenes were a popular subject for stumpwork panels. It would have been a common pastime for women and part of girls' education.

It was a slow and intricate form of embroidery, layering stitches and sewing on decorations such as seed pearls to create three-dimensional pictures. Stitches were made around pieces of wire to create individual features such as flower petals or insect wings and then applied to the background fabric. Alternatively, shapes were created using padding, such as layers of felt, underneath the stitches.

The examples in the Musicians' Gallery date from about 1640 and include *Moses in the bulrushes*, and a mirror surround depicting *Judith with the head of Holofernes* from the Apocrypha. Biblical figures were often depicted as Charles I and Queen Henrietta Maria and dressed in clothes of their time.

Crewelwork

A popular early 17th-century form of needlework, crewelwork was essentially a form of free embroidery, only regulated by the pattern drawn onto the fabric. Jacobean designs were usually stylised floral and animal designs with vines and leaves. Like stumpwork, the stitches often created a raised, three-dimensional and textured effect. The crewelwork curtains in the adjacent Court Chamber were originally made in the 19th century, but were later remounted on to the plain linen background.

Left *Moses in the bulrushes*; mid- or late 17th-century English embroidery

20TH-CENTURY TRERICE

THE COURT CHAMBER, BATHROOM, NORTH CHAMBER, MORNING ROOM AND SHOP

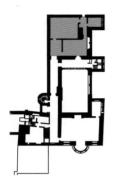

Tradition has it that on a stormy night in the 1860s the dilapidated northern end of Trerice, which had been used as storage space for the farm, collapsed. It was thought easiest to demolish the wing rather than to rebuild, and it remained like this until the National Trust bought the property in 1953. Through the generosity and enthusiasm of Mr Elton and his family, who were the resident tenants at the time, the wing was restored, as was much of the wooden flooring upstairs. Today, these restored upstairs rooms are presented to visitors in 20th-century styles, rather than the original Elizabethan era of the house.

The Landing

Hanging above the stairs is the heraldic banner of William Arundell Harris Arundell, painted on silk, dating from 1817, when he was sheriff of Cornwall. Harris Arundell was a distant descendant of Sir John 'Jack of Tilbury' Arundell, through Robert Arundell of Menadarva, who was Sir John's son by Juliana Erisey and brother to the rebuilder of Trerice.

Trerice in 1819

The watercolour shows the outside wall of the northern end of the house before it collapsed. A door on the upper storey, in a similar position to the present north door, is accessed from outside by an earthen ramp. Along that wall can also be seen possible remnants of doorways and fireplaces, suggesting that this exterior wall was once an interior wall of a long disappeared wing of the house. It seems likely that there was a wing where the raised grassy walk is now situated, mirroring the wing on the southern side and creating the impression of a large courtyard, made of two squared horseshoes, with the farm buildings.

Where were the kitchen and servants' quarters?

It is possible that they were in the earlier part the building to the north-west of the Drawing Room, or in the section of the house rebuilt in the 1950s and now occupied by the Shop – but this area was probably a high-status parlour for the family.

Right The banner flown by William Arundell Harris Arundell in 1817, when he was sheriff of Cornwall

Below Jack Elton

Below right The north wing being rebuilt in 1956

THE GARDEN

The Orchard and Knot Garden

The site of the Orchard and Knot Garden has changed drastically over the years. It has been identified as the lowermost of a suite of three Elizabethan garden terraces stepping up the hillside to the front of Trerice. This archaeology is thought to be of national significance. During the 18th and 19th centuries there was a kitchen garden in the section of this terrace adjacent to the lane, which was later remodelled as a small orchard. Photographs from the early 20th century show a well-developed Dutch ornamental garden, obviously designed to complement the house.

By the middle of the century it had been transformed into a rolling lawn, with a tennis court at the east end.

In the 1960s, the National Trust planted fruit trees, including old varieties of Cornish apples, medlars and old English apples, including the 'Flower of Kent', which is said to have helped Sir Isaac Newton discover gravity. They were varieties likely to have been grown in the estate's orchards in previous centuries. The Knot Garden was planted in 2014, on the site of the earlier Dutch garden, recreating a formal garden based on the plasterwork design of the Great Chamber ceiling.

The garden in Tudor times

Inspiration for the modern Knot Garden comes from research that this area would have been the site of a formal ornamental Tudor garden, which was an essential part of a gentleman's estate in those times. Visitors can now experience the garden as the Tudor Arundells may have; the windows of the Great Chamber provide a good view of the garden, laid out with intertwining low hedges of shrubs and herbs in geometric patterns. The garden would have been in a sunken area with a raised walk around it, traces of which can still be seen. The garden may have been expanded further east and mirrored the design of the sunken area. Near the modern summer-house was possibly a pond or water feature fed by the leat which also serviced the tunnels flushing the garderobes (toilets) in the house.

The Tudor garden, included flowers, herbs, shrubs, fruiting trees and bushes, and fashionable trees such as sycamores. William Carnsew and Richard Carew note that pears, plums, grapes, cherries, hops and quinces were grown at the time in Cornwall. Carew wrote that in Cornwall 'the gentlemen step not far behind those of other parts, many of them conceiving like to delight to graft and plant, and the soil yielding itself ready to conceive and foster'.

Below Design for a Tudor maze from Thomas Hill's *The Gardener's Labyrinth*

The Front Court

The Front Court would originally have been planted in a geometric pattern and may have included a pond. It was once partly cobbled and it was possibly paved during the 17th century and used for drilling Royalist troops in the Civil War.

By the 1950s the Front Court or 'Hall Court' was congested with large conifers and cypress trees. It was at this point that the Front Court was split into two levels with steps at the change of level, and the yew trees planted in front of the house. The crouching granite Arundell lions at the top of the steps were originally from Kenegie, the Harris Arundell property at Gluval, near Penzance, and were taken to Lifton in Devon, in the early 19th century by William Arundell Harris Arundell, who was sheriff of Cornwall in 1817. They were brought to Trerice in 1973. The steps up to the Bowling Green were also added in the 1950s.

The Front Court may once have had a gatehouse on the roadside, aligned with the porch of the house. The present ornamental gate was installed in the 1970s; the granite caps and balls of the gate-piers were brought to Trerice from Tresmarrow, near Launceston, after it was demolished in 1975 to make way for the Launceston bypass.

The present arrangement of the paths probably echoes the original layout. Those that have disappeared under the turf include one that ran along the southern wall eastwards and passed a gap in the wall between the Front Court and garden. There may even have been an earlier broad walk to the north, similar to the one above the Orchard and Knot Garden. The 1825 estate survey lists 'the house, with courtyard and Lady's Garden' (thought to be

Above The Front Court with the Arundell lions

Left The Knot Garden

the Front Court), suggesting the ornamental character of the area. The 'Lady's Garden' would have been in existence by 1698, when the inventory refers to 'My Lady's Chamber', which possibly overlooked this site.

THE KAYLING LAWN

The top terrace, a bowling green now known as the kayling lawn, provides a good position for close up inspection of the Dutch-influenced façade of the house. Bowling became so popular that by 1542 it was restricted to the gentry with a landed income of over £100 a year. By this law, bowling, as well as tennis, cards, dice and backgammon, was confined to a gentleman's property. Consequently, a bowling green became a fashionable area of the garden as well as a status symbol. There are traces of a viewing mount in the north-east corner, an ideal place for Tudor ladies to watch the game. Around the edge of the green would have been an ornamental garden, with borders of fruit trees.

The 1698 inventory mentions a 'Bowling Green Chamber' in the house, which suggests that it overlooked the green and was possibly in the north wing, which has long since disappeared.

William Carnsew, a son-in-law to John Arundell V, the rebuilder of Trerice, was enthusiastic about outdoor games and gambling, and records in his diary from the 1570s that he often played bowls. Surprisingly, he does not mention playing at Trerice, where he was a frequent visitor, though he played with the Arundell family at Lanherne. The remains of farm buildings along the north-west side suggest that the kayling lawn was given over to the farm by the 19th century.

The Parade Ground and Mowhay

The Parade Ground gets its name from the period in the Second World War when the Home Guard was stationed at Trerice (see p.30). The ground had been levelled in the early 19th century to create a mowhay to store hayricks. It was used as a grass tennis court in the 1920s.

Kayles

Early 20th century photographs of Trerice show a game of skittles or Cornish 'kayles' set up outside the front door. The set of turned baluster-shaped oak ninepins in the Great Hall is 16th-century. The ball is nicknamed the 'cheese'.

Kayling was played in England in the 14th century and has been indigenous to Cornwall for at least 500 years, though it possibly originates from France. It was also played by throwing a stick at the pins rather than a ball and with the pins in a straight line. In 1366 Edward III outlawed bowling because it distracted men from archery practice. A popular sport to gamble on, bowling was considered a game only for the wealthy who needed to have a licence for a private bowling green. In contrast, Richard Carew, writing in the late 16th century, comments that kayles was a game often played by miners.

Trerice Manor House near Newquay.

THE ESTATE

The Great Barn

The outbuildings form a U-shaped complex, mirroring the original Tudor house layout. The Great Barn in the centre (now the restaurant) was used to store and process crops from the fields, with housing underneath for animals. When open, the parallel doorways would have provided an excellent site to thresh the corn, using the draught created to take away the chaff.

On the north side (now the restaurant kitchen) was a large stable for farm horses, with a barn or storage area above. To the south, on the end of the barn was a cider mill, used to crush the plentiful crop of apples from the estate orchards, with a single-storey stable block next to it.

A leat provided the water power to drive the grinding mill, and in the 19th century was used to power the machinery for chaff-cutting, mangold-slicing, winnowing and feed-mixing.

The farm, due to its close proximity to the house, reminds us of the ultimate source of the Arundells' wealth and power in land. The sale catalogue of 1915 claims that the farm at Trerice was 'reputed to be one of the best in Cornwall', and at this time it was one of the largest in St Newlyn East parish.

The Farmyard Terrace

A Tudor-style garden has been laid out on the lower terrace behind the Great Barn. It began as a joint project with St Newlyn East Primary School to grow herbs and vegetables based on *The Gardener's Labyrinth* (1577), such as purple carrots (an authentic feature of a Tudor vegetable garden) and plants used for medicinal purposes. Items now grown in the beds are occasionally used in the restaurant's dishes.

Below the ground still remain the foundations of the courtyard farm buildings demolished in the early 20th century. A corner of the building was discovered during work to install a gas pipeline in 2005. The lower corner of this area overlooks the green lane leading down to the ford, which is the reason for Trerice being here and gives the property its name.

A pocket park

The modern car-park covers part of the old Outer Orchard, which would have provided the Acland family with a large apple crop for the cider mill. It was one of several orchards; the Little Orchard was to the west, and the Walk Orchard across the road to the east.

Above A sketch of the Great Barn in 1824 by Sir Thomas Dyke Acland

These may have been extensions of the ornamental garden areas of Tudor and Stuart Trerice.

Beyond the car-park towards the bottom of the valley is The Wilderness, currently inaccessible to visitors. Here there are the remains of dried-up lakes, and possibly a 17th century or earlier fish pond. In the 18th century this was expanded to create a system of lakes, with ornamental islands and stepping stones, which were part of the redesigned parkland. This designed landscape originally stretched both upstream and downstream of the section now owned by the National Trust. In the 1920s a hydraulic ram was installed to pump water from the stream to the top of the gardens.

By the dating of trees popular at the time, such as limes and sycamores, it has been established that the parkland was probably planted between 1720 and 1760.

Fields in the wider estate
The names given to fields around Trerice indicate their purpose, such as Beef Close, Sheep Meadow and Horse Close. Warren Field suggests the keeping and breeding of rabbits, and Culver Close suggests the presence of a dovecote. The field opposite the Front Court at Trerice, across the road, was named Chapel Close, indicating that this was the site of the chapel for

which licences were granted in the 14th and 15th centuries.

Across the valley from Trerice is Prick Close, which gets its name from the fixed target used in archery, or the bull's eye. Archery was a popular sport and pastime in the 16th century, not least because of its military uses. The distance used in practices was usually 240 paces (a twelve-score prick) or 480 paces. Carew recorded the popularity of archery in his 1602 *Survey of Cornwall*, and to mark the prowess of Cornishmen noted '*one Master Robert Arundell (whom I well knew) could shoot twelve score, with his right hand, with his left, and from behind his head*'. 'Master Robert' was Robert Arundell of Menadarva, and one wonders whether he may have practised at Trerice; the distance between the medieval terrace walk and Prick Close is 240 paces.

Below A coloured postcard of Trewerry Mill built by Sir John Arundell VI in 1639 to serve the Trerice estate

Trewerry Mill near Newquay

THE ARUNDELLS OF TRERICE

The name Arundell is thought to be French in origin. This is reflected in the family's coat of arms, which features six swallows, a pun on the French word for swallow, 'hirondelle'. By the 16th century, the Arundell family had become well-established and was connected by marriage to nearly all the other landed families in the county.

Left Mary Bevill, Jack of Tilbury's first wife

Centre Jack of Tilbury; a replica of his tomb brass in St Andrew's Church, Stratton

Right Juliana Erisey, Jack of Tilbury's second wife

Ralph Arundell of Caerhays married Jane Trerise in the early 14th century, and through her, inherited Trerice. When Ralph died in the late 1360s, his son Nicholas was possibly still a minor. He was abducted from his guardian John Tynton by William Lambourn and his wife Joan, who in 1372 applied for a licence for a private chapel at Trerice.

Successive generations increased the family's status by working for the Crown in the county and through good marriages. John Arundell I married Jane Durant in the early 15th century and gained Ebbingford Manor near Bude as part of her dowry. In the 1420s he held the position of household steward of the Earl of Huntingdon, was vice-admiral of Cornwall, and was the first of his family to be a Member of Parliament.

JOHN ARUNDELL II

According to tradition, around the 1460s John II was told by a shepherd he had convicted that 'when upon the yellow sand, thou shall die by human hand'. In order to avoid fulfilling this prophecy, Arundell moved to Trerice from Ebbingford. Legend goes that in 1471, while sheriff of Cornwall, he was ordered to regain St Michael's Mount from the Lancastrian earl of Oxford who had fled there after the battle of Barnet. Arundell attempted to take the Mount by force but was killed on the beach at Marazion.

Recent research at Trerice has found that the siege of the Mount actually took place in 1473, coinciding with the death of Sir John Arundell of Lanherne. Arundell of Trerice was forced to quit Ebbingford because Edward IV gave the manor to the Fulfords. There are no surviving records showing when exactly John II died.

'JACK OF TILBURY': SIR JOHN ARUNDELL IV

John II's grandson, known as 'Jack of Tilbury', was knighted in 1542 for services to the Crown. Among his many exploits, in 1523 Arundell received thanks from the King for his 'valiant courage and bold enterprise' used to capture Duncan Campbell, a notorious Scottish pirate after a fight at sea.

In 1536 Jack of Tilbury led one of four Cornish companies in the north to counter the Pilgrimage of Grace. At the head of a company of 40 men, he helped to quell the serious rebellion against the King's authority. It is generally thought that the Trerice Arundells where Protestant supporters, while the Lanherne branch were noted Catholics. The Arundel coat of arms in the Great Chamber suggests Catholic sympathies, and it seems likely that the Trerice Arundells put loyalty to the Crown before religious beliefs.

In 1537 Arundell wrote to the king reporting the inadequacy of Cornwall's coastal defences. Spanish and French ships, then at war with each other, sailed up the river at Falmouth, and the Spanish chased the French as far as Truro, despite Arundell's threats to raise the local people in defence. He wrote of his desire for *the King's help to have blockhouses made upon our haven, else we shall have more of this business*. This, combined with the threat of invasion once France and Spain made peace in 1539, led to the building of Pendennis and St Mawes castles, which were completed in the mid-1540s. Arundell was made vice-admiral of the western seas under Edward VI.

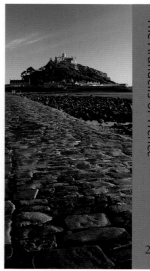

Above St Michael's Mount, where, legend has it, Sir John Arundell II was killed

THE REBUILDER OF TRERICE: JOHN ARUNDELL V

At the death of Jack of Tilbury in 1560, it was unclear who would inherit Trerice. Through his first marriage to Mary Bevill, he had three children, including a son, Roger, but on his death Trerice and his main estates went to John V, his son by his second wife Juliana Erisey. Roger had died during his father's lifetime, but Roger's own son, another John, did not inherit Trerice, which provoked a dispute with his cousin and namesake. This was finally settled in 1610, when John Arundell VI of Trerice resorted to Parliament, and an act was passed stating that Roger had been a lunatic, which barred his children from inheriting the Trerice estate.

The John Arundell who succeeded to Trerice is known as the rebuilder of Trerice. He was the second son of his father's second marriage: his elder brother Robert was born before his parents married and was never properly legitimised, though he was treated as a full member of the family and inherited the Menadarva estate.

In 1562 John Arundell married Katherine Hill (née Cosworth), daughter of John Cosworth. Cosworth granted his lands to Arundell and was to pay £40 a year for four years, followed by £60 a year thereafter; in return for which, he, and his wife and servants were entitled to live at Trerice with free board and lodging for the rest of their lives. In 1572, the year the Great Hall was finished, Katherine died, leaving Arundell with four young daughters. He was married again, to Gertrude Denys, the following year.

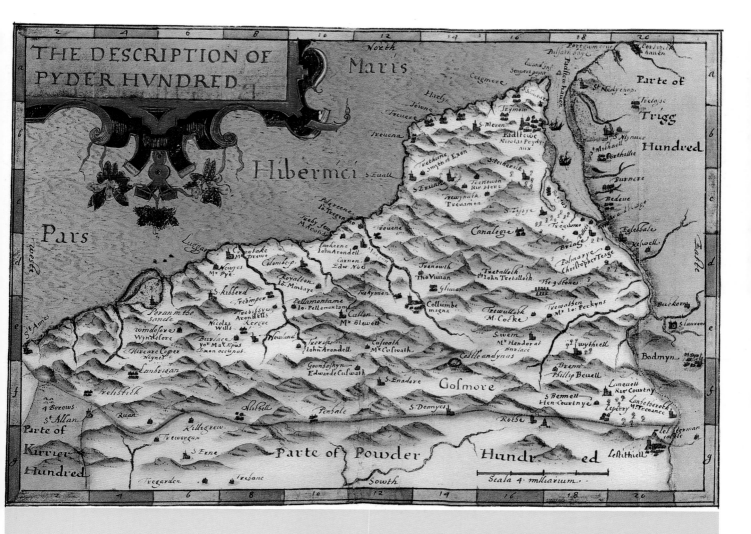

THE DESCRIPTION OF PYDER HVNDRED

A black sheep

Robert Arundell of Menadarva, a skilled archer, was a black sheep of the family. He was taken to court for cattle rustling and narrowly escaped execution. He was later outlawed and imprisoned for not paying his debts and in 1561 was ordered to pay one John Trelawney 1,000 marks for slander: he and his servant were described as 'two as light and wanton persons of their behaviour and conversation as is in Cornwall and very much dreaded and feared'.

Above John Norden's *c.*1597 map of north Cornwall includes Trerice

Opposite John Arundell V, who rebuilt Trerice in the 1570s, is flanked by his brothers Roger and Richard on this tomb brass

Above The Earl of Strafford

Below A Civil War
re-enactment at Trerice

'JOHN FOR THE KING': JOHN ARUNDELL VI

In 1580 John Arundell V died at the age of 46 and was succeeded by his son John, aged nearly four, who later became known as 'John for the King'. According to Carew, the younger John, 'even from his young years, began where his father left, and with so temperate a course treadeth just in his footsteps, that he inheriteth as well his love as his living'.

'John for the King' is most widely known for his role in the Civil War, especially his defence of Pendennis Castle for Charles I. Peter Courtenay commented on the trial of the Earl of Strafford, in 1640: *'My Cousin Arundell is very Angry with his son Richard for voting him not guilty of treason'*. Strafford had been a leading adviser to Charles I, who later turned against him, and this was the first time support for the King and opposition to parliamentary reform was shown by Cornish MPs. In June 1642 a group of Royalist supporters drew up a petition in Lostwithiel and John Arundell was among the 7,000 signatories. It soon became clear that the Cornish gentry would have to decide whether they supported the King or Parliament; the Trerice Arundells supported the King.

In 1643 John Arundell took over the command of Pendennis Castle. Arundell's eldest son, John, was killed leading Royalist troops at Plymouth in the same year, while two of his other sons, Richard and Nicholas, served at Pendennis and saw action at Edgehill and Landsdowne. In 1644, not long after Arundell took command, Queen Henrietta Maria stayed overnight at the castle as she fled the country to France.

On 18 March 1646 General Fairfax, who had been blockading the Royalists in the castle, had demanded their surrender. Arundell quickly responded:

The castle was committed to my government by His Majesty, who by our laws hath the command of castles and forts of the Kingdom, and my age of seventy summons me hence shortly. Yet I shall desire no testimony to follow my departure than my conscience to God and loyalty to His Majesty, whereto I am bound by all the obligations of nature, duty and oath. I wonder you demand the castle without authority from His Majesty, which if I should render, I brand myself and my posterity with the indelible character of Treason. And having taken less than two minutes resolution, I resolve that I will here bury myself before I deliver up this castle to such as fight against His Majesty, and that nothing you can threaten is formidable to me in respect of loss of loyalty and conscience.

On 11 April Arundell reported to Prince Charles that his men were unwilling to work unpaid and he lacked the means to pay them. He observed that the enemy had rather successfully blockaded the castle from Arwennack, from where they were in range of cannon shot. He added that he only had six weeks worth of provisions left and asked for £200 and stores including clothing, medicine, food, munitions and weapons, and 2000lb of tobacco and '20 gross of pipes' to smoke the tobacco.

On 17 April Arundell received another demand for surrender, which again he defiantly turned down. By 27 June Arundell reported to Prince Charles in Jersey that *'it is now come to the last with us, and this place which you and your Father's whole interest in the West must be necessarily so ruined within three weeks…we urge nothing for ourselves, nor the rest of your loyal servants here who are now poorly clothed, and sickly fed upon bread and water…'*

The garrison held out until 17 August. The survivors consisted of 24 officers and 900 men; the terms granted to them were seen as generous and included £500 for the sick and wounded and food provisions for the defeated garrison's homeward march. Many of the garrison later died due to the privations they had suffered.

The Arundells continued to resist the Parliamentarian rule and were among the ringleaders of an uprising plotted in 1648. As a result, John Arundell was arrested, and his estate was sequestered; he was ordered to pay a £10,000 fine (almost £1,000,000 today), though this was later reduced to £2,000. Arundell was considered 'one of the most irreconcilable' Royalists in Cornwall. After John Arundell's death in 1656, his son Richard plotted another uprising with other Cornish Royalists, but it was discovered by Parliamentarians, when arms they had gathered were taken to a local blacksmith for repair.

Below left Pendennis Castle under siege in 1646. A bird's-eye view reconstruction by Alan Sorrell

Below Charles I, whose cause was upheld in the West Country by 'John for the King'

27

whose charms were not equal to her fortune'. He married Margaret Acland, daughter of Sir John Acland of Columb-John in Devon, through whom the Aclands later inherited Trerice. On his death in 1698 his widow and second wife, Barbara Arundell, drew up an inventory of the contents of Trerice, which reveals the large number of rooms in the house at this period and the extent of the farm.

In 1698 the 2nd Baron was succeeded by his son, another John, who died nine years later aged 28. It was rumoured that he starved himself for love of a lady who rejected him. The 4th Baron inherited the title in 1706, when he was only five. On his death in 1768, the Arundell line died out, and Trerice passed to his late wife's nephew, William Wentworth.

Above Richard Arundell was ennobled by Charles II in 1664/5 in gratitude for his father's loyalty to the Crown during the Civil War. The Patent granting him a barony hangs in the Gallery

Right John, 3rd Lord Arundell as a boy

THE BARONS ARUNDELL

After the restoration of Charles II, Richard Arundell was created Baron Arundell of Trerice in 1664/5 for his support of Charles I. He was given an annual pension of £1,000 in 1674, plus £2,000 per annum from excise and £20,000 from boons.

John, 2nd Baron Arundell, succeeded his father in 1687. He was MP for Truro at the age of seventeen and was described as *'of great loyalty and integrity, and a person whom envy itself cannot blemish in the least'*. He once duelled over an heiress and twice wounded his rival *'after which he closeth with him and with his Cornish dexterity throws him flat on his back, takes away his sword and breaks it; and then gives him his life, and his mistress,*

LATER HISTORY

ABSENTEE LANDLORDS

Wentworth was the first of several generations of absentee landlords, his home estate being Henbury in Dorset. The manor house and home farm were leased to tenants, who made few changes to them.

William's son, Frederick Thomas, inherited Trerice in 1775. He died without offspring in 1799, and bequeathed Trerice to his sister Augusta Ann Hatfield Kaye of Hatfield Hall, Yorkshire, who was by this time in her 60s. In 1802 Trerice passed to Sir Thomas Dyke Acland, 10th Bt, of Columb-John and Killerton, in accordance with the last Baron Arundell's will.

When the Acland family visited Cornwall in the summer, they usually stayed in Bude, as it was closer to their Devon estates than Trerice. The manors of Ebbingford (Efford) and Thurlibeer, near Bude, became increasingly important to the Aclands due to their revived interest in constructing a canal linking Bude to the Tamar, which opened in 1823. However, Sir Thomas did visit Trerice occasionally and held gatherings in the Great Hall for family, tenants and workers.

For most of the 19th century, Trerice was leased to the Tremaine family. In 1841 Trerice was occupied by William Tremaine and his family. He was succeeded by his son John, who was described as a farmer of 500 acres employing twelve men, four women and four boys. Among the live-in servants was a housemaid, a dairymaid, a ploughman and two carters. It was during this time that a storm brought down the dilapidated end of the house. By 1871 John's widow, Susan,

was running the farm supported by her son William. Over the next 30 years the number of people living at Trerice decreased. In 1901 William lived there with his wife and son, Henry, and two domestic servants, indicating the continued decline of this once-great estate.

Trerice was sold in 1915, like many other old estates during and after the First World War. In 1919 Trerice was briefly owned by Cornwall County Council, which divided Trerice into twelve separate farm holdings intended for returning war veterans. The main house was sold again, with the acreage much reduced in size, to Mr C.E. Shepherd. Trerice was later bought by Somerset de Chair, a flamboyant MP and author, who sold the property to the National Trust in 1953. The Trust opened the house to the public (initially two rooms, the Great Hall and the Great Chamber) for the first time in 1954.

The subject of an illustrated article in COUNTRY LIFE.
TRERICE MANOR
One of the finest unspoilt Tudor Manor Houses in the country.

STONE-BUILT MANOR, NEAR CORNISH COAST
Many interesting period features.
Great Hall, drawing room, dining room, study, 8 bedrooms (3 with basins). Aga cooker. Central heating. Main electricity. Outbuildings. Gardens and orchard.
About 16 ACRES with possession.
FOR SALE FREEHOLD.   PRICE £15,000
Further particulars and photographs from the Sole Agents: JOHN D. WOOD & CO., 23, Berkeley Square, W.1. (70,757)

Above A Sunday school visit to Trerice around 1905

Left A *Country Life* advertisement for the 1948 sale

THE CHOUGHS

During the Second World War Trerice was used as a base for the local Home Guard, the 11th Cornwall Battalion (Newquay), attached to the Duke of Cornwall's Light Infantry, which was nicknamed the Choughs. It was the headquarters of the Newlyn East 'C' Company. Each company of the battalion was originally made up from the Local Defence Volunteers, which later became the Home Guard. Basic drill was carried out on the Parade Ground. The battalion stood down in 1944 after three years of service, which included manning look-out posts at Carland Cross and Trendrean and rifle practice on Newlyn Downs. At the stand-down parade on 3 December the commanding officer Lt Col. Holman presented Mr C.E. Shepherd with a flag bearing a chough as a token of thanks for allowing the 11th Battalion to use Trerice as their training centre; in response Mr Shepherd said that the flag *would be hoisted over Trerice Manor on all appropriate occasions*.

In the months before the battalion finally stood down, poems and recollections of their experiences were recorded. The Newlyn East Choughs provided the following:

Centred on the house at Shepherds
Specialists in 'unarmed combat';
Keeping closer touch with Newquay,
Theirs to keep untiring vigil
All the way from Porth to Zelah,
Crantock, Polly Joke and Cubert,
Holywell, Penhale, Goonhavern,
Newlyn, Carnebo, Rejerrah;
Carland of the famous watch-tower;
East Wheal Rose of the Assault-course.
Where the men of the Battalion,
Thanks to Mr G.H. Johnstone,
Cornwall's Johnstone of Trewithen,
Learned to prove and use their weapons;
Famed Trerice of the Arundells,
Now the home of Mr Shepherd,
Who, with glad co-operation,
Lent his ancient barns and paddocks,
Ideal for Battalion training…

Below This silver shooting trophy of a Vickers machine gun was presented to members of the Home Guard who served at Trerice during the Second World War

Above The flag emblazoned with a Cornish chough which flew at Trerice during the summer of 1940, when the Local Defence Volunteers drilled on the Parade Ground

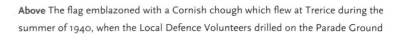

TRERICE TODAY

Today Trerice continues to develop, though keeping its quintessential and unique charm. Its role has varied considerably over the years, from hub of a large estate to a place for local Sunday School picnics in the early 20th century to a base for the Home Guard in the Second World War. Since its restoration in the 1950s, Trerice has become a place to bring the past alive. Various opportunities are now available for visitors to explore the past in a tangible way, from newly acquired replica items – such as Tudor clothes, armour, toys and games – to magical Christmases.

Surveys of the garden, parkland and buildings by the County Council's archaeological team now make it possible to better understand how each part of Trerice was used over the centuries – how the buildings changed and interacted with each other. Hidden gems brought to light have spurred on further investigation, creating new perspectives on old ideas, and leading to new discoveries and rediscovering forgotten knowledge – whether in the garden, the house, the collection or about the families that lived here.

The renowned stillness and tranquillity of Trerice is now occasionally pierced by raucous music or shouts of excitement from the kayling lawn bringing back some of the bustle and noise that must have typified its time as a busy manor house. Trerice is no longer a place where the past is quietly enshrined; it is a place where history is actively brought to life, allowing all the features of life at Trerice and of the people who lived there to be fully appreciated.

Above A costume day at Trerice

THE ARUNDELLS OF TRERICE

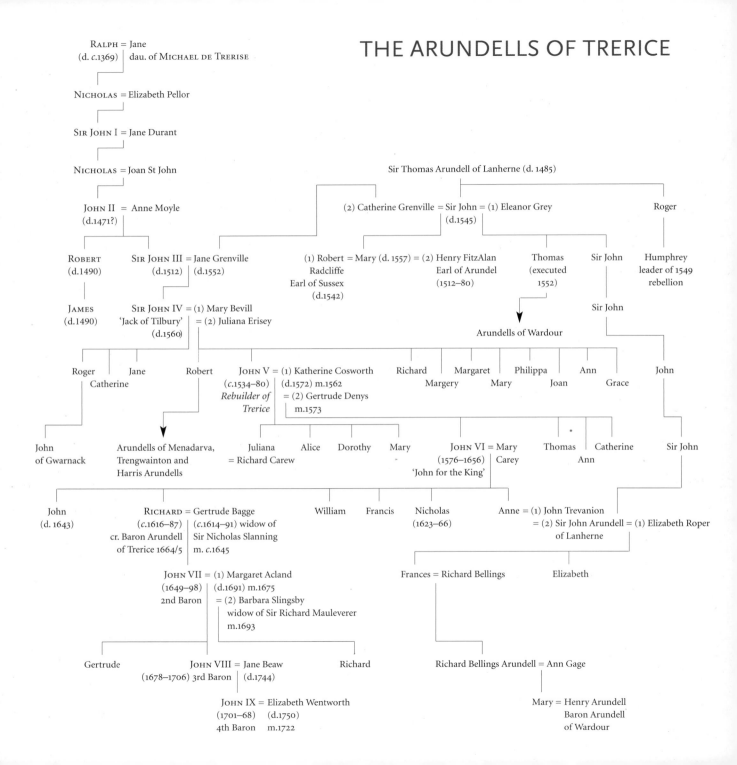

Ralph = Jane
(d. c.1369) | dau. of Michael de Trerise

Nicholas = Elizabeth Pellor

Sir John I = Jane Durant

Nicholas = Joan St John

Sir Thomas Arundell of Lanherne (d. 1485)

John II = Anne Moyle
(d.1471?)

(2) Catherine Grenville = Sir John = (1) Eleanor Grey   Roger
(d.1545)

Robert (d.1490)   Sir John III = Jane Grenville
(d.1512) (d.1552)

(1) Robert = Mary (d. 1557) = (2) Henry FitzAlan   Thomas   Sir John   Humphrey
Radcliffe   Earl of Arundel   (executed   leader of 1549
Earl of Sussex   (1512–80)   1552)   rebellion
(d.1542)

James (d.1490)   Sir John IV = (1) Mary Bevill
'Jack of Tilbury'
= (2) Juliana Erisey
(d.1560)

Sir John

Arundells of Wardour

Roger   Jane   Robert   John V = (1) Katherine Cosworth   Richard   Margaret   Philippa   Ann   John
Catherine   (c.1534–80)   (d.1572) m.1562   Margery   Mary   Joan   Grace
                         Rebuilder of   = (2) Gertrude Denys
                         Trerice   m.1573

John   Arundells of Menadarva,   Juliana   Alice   Dorothy   Mary   John VI = Mary   Thomas   Catherine   Sir John
of Gwarnack   Trengwainton and   = Richard Carew   (1576–1656)   Carey   Ann
              Harris Arundells   'John for the King'

John   Richard = Gertrude Bagge   William   Francis   Nicholas   Anne = (1) John Trevanion
(d. 1643)   (c.1616–87)   (c.1614–91) widow of   (1623–66)   = (2) Sir John Arundell = (1) Elizabeth Roper
cr. Baron Arundell   Sir Nicholas Slanning   of Lanherne
of Trerice 1664/5   m. c.1645

John VII = (1) Margaret Acland
(1649–98)   (d.1691) m.1675
2nd Baron   = (2) Barbara Slingsby
            widow of Sir Richard Mauleverer
            m.1693

Frances = Richard Bellings   Elizabeth

Gertrude   John VIII = Jane Beaw   Richard
(1678–1706) 3rd Baron   (d.1744)

Richard Bellings Arundell = Ann Gage

John IX = Elizabeth Wentworth
(1701–68)   (d.1750)
4th Baron   m.1722

Mary = Henry Arundell
Baron Arundell
of Wardour